D1518648

Bilingual Edition

READING POWER

Edición Bilingüe

Alexi Lalas

Soccer Sensation

Sensación del fútbol soccer

Rob Kirkpatrick

Traducción al español
Mauricio Velázquez de León

The Rosen Publishing Group's
PowerKids Press™ & Buenas Letras™
New York

For Mike, Gina and Randi from RU.
Para Mike, Gina, y Randi de parte de RU.

Published in 2002 by The Rosen Publishing Group, Inc.
29 East 21st Street, New York, NY 10010

First Bilingual Edition 2002
First Edition in English 2001

Book design: Maria Melendez

Photo Credits: p. 5 © Jamie Squire/Allsport; p. 7 © Al Bello/Allsport; p. 9 © Brian Bahr/Allsport; p. 11 © David Silverman/MLS/Allsport; p. 13 © Michael Stahlschmidt/Allsport; p. 15 © Shaun Botterill/Allsport; p. 17 © Jamie Squire/Allsport; p. 19 © Todd Warshaw/Allsport; p. 21 © Rick Stewart/Allsport; p. 22 © Sportsphoto.

Text Consultant: Linda J. Kirkpatrick, Reading Specialist/Reading Recovery Teacher

Kirkpatrick, Rob.
  Alexi Lalas : soccer sensation = Alexi Lalas : sensación de fútbol soccer / by Rob Kirkpatrick : traducción al español Mauricio Velázquez de León.
    p. cm. — (Reading power)
    Includes index.
    Summary: Introduces the soccer star, Alexi Lalas.
    ISBN 0-8239-6137-0
    1. Lalas, Alexi—Juvenile literature. 2. Soccer players—United States—Biography—Juvenile literature. [1. Lalas, Alexi. 2. Soccer players. 3. Spanish language materials—Bilingual.] I. Title. II. Series.
    GV942.7.L35 K57 1999
    796.334'092—dc21
    [B]

Word Count:
English: 132
Spanish: 143

Manufactured in the United States of America

Contents

1 Meet Alexi Lalas   4
2 Head the Ball   8
3 Goals   12
4 Winning   14
5 Books and Web Sites   23
6 Glossary   24
7 Index   24

Contenido

1 Conoce a Alexi Lalas   4
2 Cabecear el balón   8
3 Goles   12
4 Ganando partidos   14
5 Libros y páginas en Internet   23
6 Glosario   24
7 Índice   24

Alexi Lalas plays soccer.

———

Alexi Lalas juega
fútbol soccer.

Soccer players have to run a lot. Alexi has to run a lot in games.

Los jugadores de fútbol soccer tienen que correr mucho. Alexi corre mucho durante los partidos.

Alexi can hit the ball with his head. He can do this when the ball is in the air.

———

Alexi puede golpear el balón con la cabeza. Él cabecea el balón cuando se encuentra en el aire.

Alexi has played for the Revolution. They have red, white, and blue shirts.

—————

Alexi ha jugado en el equipo *Revolution*. Las camisetas de este equipo tienen los colores rojo, blanco y azul.

Alexi played for the Metro Stars. He liked to score goals for them. It made him happy.

———

Alexi jugó con los *Metro Stars*. Alexi se ponía muy feliz cuando anotaba goles para su equipo.

13

Alexi plays for the United States. He helps them win. Alexi and the other players are happy when they win.

Alexi juega en la selección de los Estados Unidos. Él los ayuda a ganar. Alexi y los otros jugadores se ponen felices cuando ganan.

Alexi has red hair.

———————

Alexi es pelirrojo.

Alexi's hair was long. He got his hair cut. Now Alexi's hair is short.

———

El cabello de Alexi era largo. Ahora le gusta llevarlo más corto.

Alexi likes soccer. He likes music, too. He plays the guitar.

———————

A Alexi le gusta el fútbol soccer. Pero también le gusta la música. Toca la guitarra.

Alexi went to Italy to play soccer. Players in Italy are very good. Alexi is good, too.

Alexi jugó fútbol en Italia. Los jugadores en Italia son muy buenos, como Alexi.

Here are more books to read about soccer:
Para leer más acerca de fútbol soccer, te recomedamos estos libros:

Soccer Game! (Hello Reader!)
by Grace MacCarone,
illustrated by Meredith Johnson.
Scholastic Trade (1994)

This Is Soccer
by Margaret Blackstone,
illustrated by John O'Brien.
Henry Holt & Company, Inc.

To learn more about soccer, check out this Web site:
Para aprender más sobre soccer, visita este Web site:

http://sportsline.netscape.com/ns/soccer/index/html

23

Glossary

games (GAYMZ) When two teams play.

goal (GOHL) When you put the ball in the other team's net. Your team gets one point for a goal.

guitar (gih–TAR) A thing that you play to make music.

players (PLAY-erz) People like Alexi who are in games.

score (SKOR) To get a point for your team.

Index

B
ball, 8
G
games, 6
goals, 12
guitar, 20

I
Italy, 22
M
Metro Stars, 12

P
players, 6, 14, 22
R
Revolution, 10
S
score, 12

Glosario

anotación Conseguir un gol para tu equipo.

gol Cuando metes el balón en la portería del otro equipo. Tu equipo obtiene un punto por cada gol.

jugador, a Personas como Alexi que participan en los partidos.

partido (el) Cuando dos equipos juegan fútbol soccer.

selección (la) Equipo que representa a un país en competiciones internacionales.

Índice

A
anotación, 12
B
balón, 8

G
goles, 12
guitarra, 20
I
Italia, 22

J
juegos, 6
jugadores, 6, 14, 22
M
Metro Stars, 12
R
Revolution, 10